My Multiverse

Kathleen Halme

New Issues Poetry & Prose

A Green Rose Book

New Issues Poetry & Prose
The College of Arts and Sciences
Western Michigan University
Kalamazoo, Michigan 49008

First Edition, 2015.

ISBN: 978-1-936970-31-5 (paperbound)

Library of Congress Cataloging-in-Publication Data:
Halme, Kathleen.
My Multiverse/Kathleen Halme
Library of Congress Control Number: 2014952970

Editor: William Olsen
Managing Editor: Kimberly Kolbe
Layout Editor: McKenzie Lynn Tozan
Assistant Editor: Alyssa Jewell
Art Direction: Nicholas Kuder
Design: Mariesa DeSantis
Production: Paul Sizer
                   The Design Center, Frostic School of Art
                   College of Fine Arts
                   Western Michigan University
Printing: McNaughton & Gunn, Inc.

My Multiverse

Kathleen Halme

New Issues

WESTERN MICHIGAN UNIVERSITY

Also by Kathleen Halme

For Pentti Kalevi Halme

Contents

VI. The Reader Became the Book

City of Roses

City of Roses

I.

Dear,
come away from the screen.
Wildebeests and baboons with babies
will keep drinking from the water hole.
Don't they ever turn off the camera?

"Now the sun is coming up,
listen to those birds!"

Here we are, a time being.
Eden of the West.
Rain gray West. On our nurse log
grow gold mushrooms, sword ferns, emerald moss.
Here we go loopty loo.

Story is the absorption
that we live. A spirit's experiment
married to a brain.

I'm scrubbing off some DNA,
a hundred years of pushing on a door.
The grime is thickest near the knob.

A strand of DNA is 2.5 nanometers wide.
A nanometer is a billionth of a meter.
Does this seem mundane?
We are all infinitely interesting,
then there is the world—the inner
city's aggregate
of intricate particulars.
Here's the world in rain.
Leave or learn
to crave its pulsing.

Tilled earth is tilth,

taking power back,
meeting basic needs.
You think we're green?

Her rain barrel, her red worms eating peels.
Her rabbits' soft hair and meat.
Her socks from her sheep.
Her cotton glad rag.
Tilth is tilling, turning, not filth.
Permaculture is practice.
She is hoping for a confluence
of influence and being.
She would rather pick up
sticks than turn on oil heat.

We, the anthropological
in a post-Christian mode:
saints who watch the bike lane
to let the cyclists pass.

We bring home exfoliations:
a little table on wheels (we'll replace the blistered top),
a wooden radio built into a nightstand with a coin slot,
a futon frame (we'll have a mattress
made at that little shop).
Never confuse a fine-tuned consumer.

Blocks and blocks of ornate iron-fronted buildings.
Shanghai traps and tunnels.
Iron horse rings to which someone
has hitched tiny plastic palominos.

A hundred years ago this town had tribes.
Premoderns had a life
of style and stories.
What mattered to our ancestors
is called a waste of time today.

A timber baron installed lovely bronze bubblers,

hoping his mill workers would stay sober
if they had water nearby.

My neighbor collects dryer lint,
candle stubs and paper egg cartons.
He melts the wax, stirs in the beard of lint
and pours the slurry into egg compartments.
For winter solstice he brought me
a log and a sack of fire starters.
This is a form of coolness.
What sustains us shouldn't ruin us.
How do you like your life?

Green city, surly city,
unnerved by dark immersion,
City of Roses,
big and fluid as a god.

II.

Rose City. City of Roses.
They Englished it.
We live with floriferousness.

The bud pinched to a sullen pout.
The flubbed brown swabs,
caramelized roses, not sick roses,
moping roses.
In early December a few live roses.
Red one near the rock wall,
white one warming on the kitchen window,
pink ruffly one, a nervous breakdown of a rose.

Beige muzzles of roses,
rotten roses, domes and pixie hats and
the bright girls of spring:

Diadem
Sea Pearl
Gay Princess
Climbing Madame Chatenay
Mermaid
Mutablis
Opaline
Lady Waterlow
Cymbeline

Clumsy me,
I spilled a glass of water and the names washed off the page,
a blue pool on the blotter. Outside it's raining
as if it wants to spear itself inside.
I force myself outdoors.

Nuzzling the big wet roses, I'm drenched.
Rain does not saturate the fairy ones and sour.
Pink is candy lipstick, yellow is melon.
These roses smell like roses.

III.

On the hottest night in the city's brief
recorded history, in the dog days of dresses,
Ms. Kitten Heel and Ms. Nesting Box
go downtown to shop for party dresses—
to dethink an evening's heat.
They dodge the protestors'
tragic photos of the bombed.
These two friends are as real as anyone.
Feminine feminists, tonight they feel a bit frivolous.

"What do you call this?" she asks the clerk,
pinching the crinoline on a little strapless number
with a skirt that billows like petals.
"A dream. I think you could get away with this."
What she wants to get away with
involves greater risk.

Worlds without ends, a multiverse
of cascading universes. Their brains
evolved too slowly for their lives.
They could up their meds to ecstasy,
a neural overdrive, but
they are growing neural pathways.

IV.

Boulders on the bank of the great river,
artery to the Pacific, pecked with markings:
ribs and bulbous eyes. Chinook. Of course
some say the petroglyphs are evidence of aliens.
At his new suburban manse,
the man dragged the rocks
and circled them into a backyard fire pit.

Elsie Pistolhead told sixteen hours
of Sahaptin stories from her brain.

Ugly was a natural head. It meant you were a slave,
your skull unflattened by a cradle board.
What we want is . . .

Art and fact.
Elegant Klickitat baskets.
Burden baskets, water baskets, buckskin platters.
When a maker died they burned her baskets.

They knew a skin soaked
in a stew of brains and sturgeon heads
was a softening. Laden.

Spruce root hat, woven tight and rainproof,
shaped like a straw volcano blown,
a nuclear stack.

The time ball women wore around their necks
held the most important movements of their lives.

For 99.9% of human history premoderns
lived in tribes of reciprocity and rules.
They had forms for feelings.
Spirit me, spirit you.
I will be done.

V.

Twenty-eight women dance in a circle,
Twenty-eight women unwatched inside
their dance of no compete.
They're growing neural pathways.

The purpose of the circle:
see and be seen.

Less than perfect selves in genome lag;
their brains evolved too slowly for their lives.
Open in the synapse,
open in the valve.
Human bodies in Lycra
engaged in making meaning.
Ancestors didn't call it exercise—
the formal world open to the core.

They are belly breathers,
sweating from the knees,
sweating out their unmet needs.
The dance of everything they are sick of,
the dance of everything that doesn't work.

Selves with souls looking for an opening.
No one here's a Sybil shriveling in a jar.
Order of the ordinary, mythopoetic you.

Between memory and imagination
every story is about
damage, absence, lack or want.
How do they absorb
into their meaning?

They are shedding everything

that doesn't work
with brains evolved
too slowly for their lives.
They of the notochord
are growing neural pathways.

VI.

I want to speak through transformed bodies.
Of forms transformed I sing.
Transform the speaking body, sing.
I sing of transformed shapes.
I sing of forms transformed.
I sing the morphing of embodied forms.
I sing the morphing of the forms.
I morph the forms I sing.

Resemblance

Resemblance

In the old story you love, a herdsman hurls a water snake
    through an evil boy's heart, then cuts him into eight
        pieces with his sword. Into the dead land's river
            he throws the parts and in a whirlpool they churn.

When he doesn't return home, the boy's mother
    is distraught. She asks the road, the moon, the sun
        for answers and only the sun will tell the truth.
            She asks the man who designed the magic mill

to build a copper rake with iron prongs and
    she rushes to death's river to dredge up the gore.
        The mother sews her son's remains:
            the veins and nerves and bones, his clothes.

Although he is whole again, he won't speak.
    He cannot find his words.
        Who will help her sew his spirit in?
            She enlists the bee, seen both as little man and bird,

to fly around the world and bring back
    honey ointments, but none will work
        to reanimate the son. The bee
            must fly to heaven and bring back god's own

honey, water, ointment with which she fills the body's
    cracks and gaps and sings him back together:
        Rise up out of sleep. Get up out of dream.
        The life force fills him. And then

she asks him what he needs,
    and although he remembers he wants
        a maiden, a girl from the north,
            she persuades him to come home, home.

The Gala Coach of Landgraf VII of Hesse-Darmstadt

why do you in the city
of minimal sublimities love
the old coach on display
in the art mausoleum
few can afford to visit

more fey than a fairy tale pulled
by six Klickitat ponies is the carriage
carved in nervy rococo
gold lion heads stick out their royal tongues
and even the leather suspension straps
are as embroidered as trousseau lingerie

you of the city of substance
over surface could get lost
in a gold leaf trance
of curves and carvings

too high for anyone to look inside
the plain interior is stained with human juices

you know the old order
of who rides who watches
from the ditch
a man sawing meat
wipes his hands lifts his child
onto his shoulders to see
the pumpkin pass

There Was a Deer Whom the Carthean Nymphs Held Sacred

—*Metamorphoses,* Ovid

I was a god in that body.
　　Out of my head grew
　　　　a splendid rack of antlers

I bore through the high streets
　　like a fine dendritic arbor.
　　　　My beloved, Cyparissus,

strung a large pearl
　　over my forelock; it bobbed
　　　　like a globe of thought.

He rode me bareback
　　or led me by a poppy bridle.
　　　　To go about was to be loved.

I was welcome in parlors and gardens.
　　Children wove me garlands
　　　　of gardenia, bleeding heart,

and the mistletoe my darling's bow
　　released from high trees.
　　　　Mothers rocking babies on porches

offered a breast to me.
　　On the day the blossoms fell,
　　　　I lay dreaming in the grove

and was taken from this life—
　　oh the horror of my beloved's error—
　　　　shot through like any being.

Scaffolding

There rose a yellow castle
with vermillion towers,

held by a scaffolding, elaborate
with ladders and platforms.

From a winch swung a wooden bucket
that could dip into the moat

we had forgotten was a river.
The construction, a great plotless labor,

could nevertheless hold humans.
Some hidden ligature kept

the planks in place, a humility
of scraps and beams, cross ties oozing sap.

No one had cast a spell the morning
the man with a miniature god

in his pocket fell backward.
The structure had shifted and

the man tumbled into the water.
In a rush and crash, boards pulled

out of beams as every bit fell
into the glass river pouring into ocean.

Here was a common castle,
an absolutely ordinary edifice,

yet how extraordinary to come upon
this mystery and watch it collapse.

Peeked

She kept dust
on the corona and wore it
to the party.

Meet me
at dusk
in the pleasance.

What is dark in me
neurotransmit.

When she pulled the knob
on the credenza door to give
her daughter the krater,
the knob fell off.

Your soul still hurts. In the face.

Big ladies in felt hats
filled the doorstep with their tracts.

Love gives into art.

The moon did not rise.

A dark section of passage
(many rounds were fired).

Sense over our lives.
Lives of sense. A blanket
woven from your sleep.

The trunk was dead and yet
inside the branches held—

inasmuch as
buds are forming
on the scaffold planks.

They prayed
to themselves.
In the grand hotel, his room
was three doors down from hers.
Bleeding under the thumbnail
where the hammer hit.

Let me run you over the border.

I write
because I don't exist.

After the Neurologists' Cocktail Party

It isn't nothing,
       but is this consciousness,
the bee bird, green silver, tracing
       the missing shape of the feeder
now removed for a refill
       of sugar syrup? Why is it sad—
the panic blur of the little guy
       flying the contours of where
the liquor bottle hung upside down
       above its fake red flower? Is he
trying to fly the missing shape into being?
       I know my amygdala brought
the thought to me that it was my thought.

Benediction: Wakefield

The old missus with the sun on her palm
        was dismissing us, hand over us.

May the peacethatpasseth . . .
        She changed into all of us.

The pointy-faced fox curled
        around her neck studied us. The fox

was lying low in the cloud, ready
        to lock on, *understanding* all of us.

A bold fox slinking through a cloud.
        Rays shot from the missus' old nimbus.

Then the sun pulled us to the ice,
        where the red stove glowed,

warming up the skating shack . . .
        shine down upon you.

In the Gogebic Range

Blood, stand fast like a wall . . .
Your place is in the heart.
The young father carried his shot son
home on his back, and he bled out.
A hunting accident.
Someone hid the gun
in the rafters of the barn,
and people left the man alone.
He took to walking the same woods
wearing brown, he got work
with the power company. Climbing
the gray poles, *Blood, stand fast like a wall . . .*
he would not wear the safety belt. The voltage
bucked him to the ground—
Your place is in the heart—
and when he came to he clambered
back up. Liquored, in blizzards,
he spun a white truck. He beat his wife
as he beat himself. *Blood, stand fast like a wall.*
This man was no fool, but he lived
like one. He always looked
beside himself even when he
rubbed you with his love—
his bristle, spice, and snuff.
This family thought it had kept secret
what everyone in the township knew.
Your place is in the heart.

Flood

Flood

Once you were trembling
outside your ruined home.
Once you were trembling
near something worth knowing.
Ash to earth,
snow to summit
melting to freshet swelling
down the mountainside.

Deep inside the core
is fire. Ice corpses in fissures
will never see the sun.

Fall, fall, the missing all,
the dark, occulted you.
What is first, form or disorder?
Color in the shape
or color in its border?

ii.

Your sleep was blank
and desolate, your sleep
refused the stream.
You doused the pain
that never brings forgetting

with a deep green tincture
pinched in droplets, bottled with a stopper—
the forest floor filtered
through cones and moss and fungi,
old man's beard waving on branches—
springs washed through duff
that only made you sadder.
How long it took
to build an order.

A river makes its mind up as it goes;
the water pushed back. In your blank sleep
the river rowed:
long lucky, long lucky,
I take what I need,
long lucky, long lucky,
your bread I will knead.
The river called back in brinks
and swells, dissolving banks.
The road from mountain to small town
coursed as an overblown river. Now the river
is the road and the road is the river.
Not far away the stream unloads
an out tide to ocean
solvable as you. And you,
who made yourself lonely, mute
as the plugged caldera,
woke in terror,
to stand on high land wrapped
in a blanket, shaky as the others with their lanterns,

watching a miniature world below
being snatched from their powers.
Standing on high land beholden to horror,
culling and ripping new orders.

iii.

Boulders dislodge like cannon shots. The living
room tilts to pop the picture window
and drops like a country falling from a map.
The river collapses
this intricate kit—
a big unthank
of unmarked pieces,
abundances tumbling, pleasances
plunging, the soaked and swelling
couches of the dead. She had
waxed the arms with beeswax,
she had darned the trouble.

Here a blue lamp hangs
corded in its own orbit bumping over puffed
pink cumulus, insulating
the weather it gave. Above,
could you see it, could you
see it above, as
a shadeless bomb, swaying upside
down, could you see it
as a censer of reason?
Come in or out, the old voice said.

iv.

She leaned into the Grand Fir. No one
was ever more undone. Gone
were her home and broom. Gone
her flower spoons and yellow quilt,
the north sky Venus in October's full-length mirror.
Gone the home she swept with a corn broom, gone
the corn broom with its small blue velvet collar.
Her common human verbs were gone.
Be, do, give, have, make, say, show, take.
Gone.

Her eye became all fovea and saw the crowd
of honey mushrooms at her feet,
how they paraded from heartwood to hardwood,
cascading like a pilgrimage.

She saw the gills drop their spores to make
a primordium that was more surface than substance.
Around the fruiting body spread the universal veil.
Its only work was pulling in
water, release, collapse,
a deliquescence of more,
more a force than a form.
The wick's last hiss then roar.

Then she turned her eye inward, remembering
the oldest poem—*life ends*—
how we got in trouble
powering the afterlife.
She wondered how love gives rise
to art when love is failure. The parent
doesn't sing, the child won't look back—
alone, the child falls in parts.

v.

I heard it being sung,
I knew how it was made.
The rain told me a story,
the rain kept making songs.

A scribe filled his conch,
and dipped his quill in the crepuscule.
A scribe in boas wrote
on folds of strangler fig paper:
The lost word will be sung,
the lost world be restored
when soul settles into structure.

Night came in alone, and yet
I would not come true.

God of the poem, god of the mountain,
god of the rivery word,
I have no mother to sing me back together,
no father to carve me a whistle
when sap rises in the spring.

Mother pushed out the gobbets
pinned to see-through wings.
Father was crushed
when the shaft caved in.

Go where your gaze is.
Clay pipe, hive light.
No godspot or goblin
becalms melancholy's ever.

Again the writer dipped his pen and wrote:
Water brash and water blister, you are
a fur-trimmed fact caught in a cosmos,

the water bearer who drops the pot
that pours into the river of why, why.

Who are you? asks the sinking pot.
I am the one you are not, not.
What lead you to death without dying?
All rivers flow downhill.

Atlatl is a perfect word,
I thought, at last flinging
a projectile of poplar and copper.
I know the world exists
without me. What is broken
lives on in debris.
I threw into the future.
It went on and on.

More words were scraped into the page:
We know the truth, we know the rules,
sang the red worms eating scraps.
You who are standing are not
dreaming. You sleep outside of sleep.
Body/soul,
body/soul,
making mind up
as you go.
How sleep
becomes you.

vi.

Grounded with crampons a crew
keeps its footing on the steep slickness
(herbarium of mosses, and sword ferns, and glistening worts).
A crew is chopping a tunnel. They are clearing
a goat path with handsaw,
with billhook, with peavey, with log saw,
with whipsaw, they are sawing their way
to everyone marooned on the mountain.
Here is the cloudberries' gold roe you love
and bright orange chanterelles gilled in pages.

By now, you must be
hearing their cadence. The air
is new with pitch and destruction; sap
smells rich on their garments. Sap
binds their implements to their palms.
Now
you hear them.
Why are you trembling?

The Manifestations of Re-endure

Osiris Rising

When the days of green sop
darkened and we were veiled
in a comforting fog, I thought again

of the small stone statue of Osiris
waking from the dead—
a body not yet emerged

from its serpentine sheath—
the piece that made everyone stare
into the glass box in the museum.

A dead man cut into parts
and sung back together by love.
Is this a miracle we crave?

Over his head, lifted in a countenance
of bliss, an electrum headdress rises
like forming thought.

He has passed through
and he is passing, this dead man
revived by words of love.

In God's Trance Hour

the universal veil
cannot be mended
when the fruiting body
rends it an orb when pricked
is sticky and honey
light is milky the present
wrapped in skin is tied with lead
bootlaces a force field of
sorrow is a water sick
demesne the universal
veil cannot be mended
when the fruiting body rends it.

Aunt Anhedonia's Parlor

Again a crow
is tatting lace
in Aunt Anhedonia's parlor.
What pushed you
to the velvet
as dusty as the panes?

Give in, give in
snaps the pendulum
below the cuckoo's cage.
Your present tense
webs melancholy's maze.
The inverse
of depression is?

You, skinflint
of the soul,
now love nothing
in this world.
Death's daughter,
what would
make you care?
The flame inside
the hiss uncurls
inside its roar.

Say goodbye god,
that trick of taking sides.
You don't have to die
just to feel alive.

Note

Somewhere there is order,
a multiverse of order.
I could have
sewed that rip in the lining
with special strong thread,
washed pillows for the refugees,
cut new gardenias to replace
the yellowed blouses collapsed
in the vase, called someone,
hoping they'd be happy
to hear from me. I

could have faced the hard time
with the fortitude of my tribe,
planted elephant garlic,
loved you through this world,
yet I took time
to assign my pocket watch, best locket,
and gems to friends and sisters,
spread the satin wedding dress
out on the big table
for the inevitable.

Now the pills are marvelous. I
feel the tremendousness of love.

Infix

Because you share my affliction and know
how askew things can get for either of us,
I want to tell you about yesterday. I drove

to the whale beach to see how easy it would be—
the walking in, a pause, the numbed going under—
on this cold water coast. The beach was empty,

save for some surfers in wet suits. In the fog
everything up close was intensified.
On the sand I saw two gulls splayed

on their backs, eviscerated but perfectly intact.
They reminded me of standards on flagpoles.
"Leave Me Alone" and "Forget Me." I know this

is depressing; please don't be scared. I'm safe. You know
how it bothers me when I obsess about what will
become memory or not. It is more chance than choice,

that which is given to the primitive brain to be dispensed
as gifts to the nerves. The lighthouse a mile offshore,
the one that is a failed columbarium, stood out in the fog

despite it being lightless, the lens smashed out years ago
by boulders riding waves into the lantern room. Now
the place is a dovecote of death—birds share the racks

inside with human ash urns. I've read the house is falling in:
the roof, the shelves, the cremains. I was poking through
the scrack and rocks hoping to find one of the glass floats

artists have hidden on the beach. Someone must find them.
I uncovered two five dollar bills in the sand and walked
to the cloth store in the village where I bought

the softest gray flannel to make a simple skirt.
I long to see you again, to see your hands.
Come, I will be joyful.

Double Claw, Drop, Sledge, and Tack

Done, done. Done, done, the hammer says
in the neighborhood of hammering.
Hundred-year-old houses should be done.

All sleep is good sleep, work to be done.
Back to the moon, back to the sun,
she's not sick, she's sleeping.

She sleeps much more than she's awake
as a way to stay alive. Done, done,
the workers pound into her dreaming.

A nail squealed out of old wood
is grief's release. Wake up, sleep head,
grab your goat head.

Trouble

Sheep or tiger,
horse or cow?
You are able
to get well.
Hurt and sick,
ache and trouble
timed to life's big
cud of now.

Take or give,
ride or plow?
Phantom limbs,
broken brow.
Which is harder,
joy or sorrow?
You are likely
to get well.

Lulls

The curl inside the circle
is the road of your green pencil.
Spheres belted with a ring
float orbs to color in.

Copper in the quartz smells
like penny's blood. The peninsula copper
was so pure it could be pounded
into any shape when dug right
from the earth. Copper bowl or bead.

Form the teepee top then bring the wool
around from back to front. Pull down
the back pole to make a small t,
pushing the live stitch onto the back pole.
When the ball is gone, rip out
your stitches and begin again.
Never make a thing.

The sweet gum pops gumballs.
Who would plant a tree loaded
with thousands of spiked bombs?
Rake the refuse, rake the rhythm.

Avians and roses embroidered
on the Guatemalan girl's mantel.
Dark blue, light blue—count the birds
perched, the deep pink roses open.
Here are your birds,
here are your flowers.

The ivory pillow with fringes
is firm and affirming.
A creamy candle has two wicks
for two minds. Breathe
until the opal light
becomes you.

$$\frac{50}{51}$$

Loose Timber

Loose Timber

What's wrecked is almost always free
and loosened from the larger order of debris.
        The sun tumbles overboard, we bestow
our knowing to the crumbling mortar.
        Drawn to water—daughter, son—floating free.
Where's the father, where's the mother
        sunk below the loot and darkened water?
Loose timber—ash and oak and cedar—
        soaked lumber floating free.

Where Does This Ship Go?

It goes wherever it blows.
Porthole, salt pork, ham can banjo.
The purser, starving, is roped to a pole;

the mast goes wherever the craft unloads.
And I wash and sweep and sew.
And I watch the star cloud's patch of home.

Folds

Straightaway, it was full summer
and much more mysterious,
for what is summer but how we are,
at last, inside the folds of ease?
A fluent evening of soft corners, blossoms, leaves—
the ordinary miracles before death reforms us.
Walls of laurel glint fresh lacquer
as we grow gods by degrees.
Now we are mantic, simple,
disarmed by the melting moon.
Starry oblates in full summer—
free in folds of ease.

Howsoever

Not the mud man lifting the grate downtown,
mud on his knees, mud on his face,
massaging muck as if he were kneading
an enormous batch of fudge.
Not the man who found a mud ring
and pushed it down his filthy finger.

Three rules of swine I learned from a state fair farmer:

"Never touch a sow on the snout."
Although it seems to be sucking
slop with its exquisitely sensitive snout,
a pig eats with its mouth. Recall the scene
where Dorothy tumbles into a squealing pen.
They'll eat her we thought.
The pigs' own worry: she'll eat what we've got.
Zeke pulls her out and Aunt Em appears,
bearing a plate of hot crullers.

"The longer the pig, the more bacon you get,"
the farmer said to the ooing crowd leaning on the pen.
You could smell the sizzle.

"Don't expect a pig to stay clean,"
she said, powdering her piglets,
kicking their little high heels,
wrestling and nippling the sow.

We love to watch the ardency of open want.
It gives us pleasure, leaning on the fence,
seeing them feed so greedily on well-earned slops.

Daydream Three

Dried writing spiders
webbed his vestibule.
Would it kill him to pick up a broom?
I banged the Victorian knocker,

a slim bronze hand
cast with an engagement ring.
A candle in a glass stays lit,
although the wax is liquid.

Last night across the street
I'd heard the new one crying.
He spun girls in poetry—
melodious lines, odious lies.

What age is this for a "maiden like herself,
translucent, lovely, shining clear?"
Inked and pierced, in leggings and a tiny skirt,
a leather bombardier;

he'd teach her how
to write a metered line.
He'd feel real poignancy,
I vowed, and banged the hammer harder.

The malignant narcissist was home.
Before he found his words,
I spun him in the foyer.
When he crashed the credenza

I stepped on his toes.
I swear to god
I never felt such clarity—
the summer powder perfect on my wings.

Who's There?

"Who's there?"
        I ask, uncool as ever, blinking
            behind a screen.
                Why write

as though we were alone
        like reinvented bees?
           Say "please come in,"
                you've sinned by sincerity.

"I'm nobody, who are you?"
        our genius sent her letter to the world.
           Perhaps she wanted company
                as consequential as a tree.

Wannabees hum pure knowing.
        Haven't you had enough?
           No rudder, no reader, no other—
                the queen of the poem always Me.

Can the subcutaneous style please a soul,
        a fit of neural drama rushed to obscurity?
           Cleverness may be momentary
                pleasure suited to the screen.

What's wondrous to an other?
        You save yourself
           then share your oxygen.
                The fictions that we . . .

Forget-Me-Not

We gave the most when less
gave way to grace.
Perhaps it's still the way
we crave, the plotted looks
and privacies, a place to hide
our hearts. When touch
was overmuch we shied—
before the age exposed
its lurid eye.

All the Books You Want

I.

It is not always necessary to resist
retelling personal experiences.
My grade school library was an empty room,
nothing on the shelves except one book,
Kak the Copper Eskimo.

The raised picture on its cover:
a polar bear terrorizes a couple of Inuit kids—
the scene is cut and raised like a scar
you revisit with your finger tip.

Kak at twelve, proving himself to the girls
in a nearby snow house, hauls home the largest pile of fat:
two-year-old blubber hacked from a dead whale,
an ugrug seal, giant, hideous, wet.

II.

Gogebic county's phone book,
listing five pages for Wakefield, my town;
Hurlbut's Illustrated Bible, Make Ahead Meals.
Tell me what to read.

III.

The day his father died my father burned the old guy's books.
Karl Marx thrown into the big flame
of Mayan Codices, the *Talmud*, *The Grapes of Wrath*,
some *Satanic Verses*, the entire library at Alexandria.

Would you prefer to be burned with the books
you write or watch them burn?

His wasn't a typical "auto da fe."
His was about embarrassment and shame.

He desperately wanted to be an American.
Poke the flames and spread the ash
on rows of new potatoes growing papery skins.

IV.

Regarding the 2003 looting and burning
of the National Library of Iraq,
Donald Rumsfeld had this to say:
"Bad things happen in life and people do loot."
It is easy to admit the inexorable arrogance
of my own country. Secure the oil ministry,
support the biblioclasm.

V.

My rushing mother writes the wrong address—
rushing, rushing in retirement—
the box is delivered to a men's boarding house.
My sign offering a reward is ignored.

What's this?
He slits the carton with his one key.
Rush of mildew, old book stink.
Every cloth cover in a foreign language.
No illustrations. These books could be about anything.

VI.

The librarian's lament: stop bringing illustrated
books of Greek and Roman statues into the bathroom.
Stop cutting out the maps. Ignore the pimp
who reads young adult while his wife turns tricks
in the parking lot. Ignore the boy
videotaping porn off the computer screen.

VII.

"Books good for baby's brain," the worker claimed,
performing a Parisian peel on the oily woman's face.

$$\frac{64}{65}$$

The Reader Became the Book

"The House Was Quiet and the World Was Calm"
—Wallace Stevens

When One Is Idle and Alone, the Embarrassments of Loneliness Are Almost Endlessly Compounded

—*Housekeeping*, Marilyn Robinson

Do birds outside shriek
their discomfort with the inner
other, the almost other
who never is alone?

A chafing soul in this deep
with others is bombarded
by the bonds of reciprocity.

Loneliness is luxury
if you can afford it.
When calm is no calamity,
it's solid company.

The little door latched
on the cuckoo's house
keeps him inside
the mechanical clock
carved from a tree.
The oak leaf
pendulum spondees
now me, now me, now me, always
in the language of our birth.

A Wave Curled and Running Up the Wet Shore Licked Robinson's Toes

—*Friday*, Michel Tournier

He remembered the moment when
every hour he thought he'd implode
with loneliness. It could kill.

Survival depends on imagination's inner others
conjured up to keep us in the tribe.

Listing hobbies, many Americans write TV,
a clear case of obstruction.
What do we most fear,
being bored or lonely?

The sea is always salty
and we are as needy as dolphins.
People always dream of wings
instead of fins. Isn't it safer in the sea?

We talk to the moon
because it resembles a face.
Who talks to the sun?

I have when lying
in the sand. I felt it
slide inside me
like I've never felt the moon.
I was alone, a girl,
perhaps I moaned—
such novelty,
the easing out of skin.

There between the Foliate Folds, I Saw a
Loose Pearl of the Size of a Small Coconut

—20,000 Leagues Under the Sea, Jules Verne

A pet pearl turning in nacre's lotion.
      A pearl for worship and passion.
Nemo/omen. Selfish.
      Revenge like the birth of a head
when the body stays inside.

A treatise on the sublime
      never confuses sincerity with style.
The coconut is marvelous
      for what it gives:
milk, meat, a bowl of human size.

Shapes of the World Not Realised

—*To the Lighthouse*, Virginia Woolf

I had some ideas,
premature but reasonable—
the first amoeba
seen below the lens
was continental drift.

A pearl of world
lapped in luster,
then the galaxies,
spilled beads—
Coma Cluster, star burst
ring, Bubble Nebula—
spark and world.

The multiverse,
do we call it nature?
The big bang waves
still hum inside our selves.

That's room enough and reason—
the mirror ball of meaning
strung without a thread.

I'm in Love with All This

—*To the Lighthouse*, Virginia Woolf

The genome's home. Kinship
is a hedge. At least she knew

what was beloved. She loved.
It occupied what little time she had.

Evolution's overrated: too slow
to save a life. She cared to know

the known. Blue cups and almond cake
inside the shrubs trimmed higher

than the eye. A pleasure party
for the equinox. "I'm in love," he said.

"With what?" she asked, sipping leaves
and flowers, free from genius.

One Who Feels Rather Than Reasons

—*Sister Carrie*, Theodore Dreiser

Reason is the deepening hologram
of a peace dove, or is it an eagle,
      winging the limited pristine,
a holding pattern that's quickly swiped.
      New plastic is an accounting—
activated, a soul feels a trembling
      in the wings, the moment's anarchy
and rush. We want beauty or we want
      to be bought by feeling.
Alone is not equal to lonely,
      fourth on the failure scale of our unreason.
Image we know, not illustration,
      confusing the dove with imaginative acts.

Stay and Play Nicely, Goddamn You

—*Fishboy*, Mark Richard

It goes like this.
"Goddamn you, play nice!" yells the mother.
She brings home used syringes,
hypodermics to engorge a bee.
The croquet mallet's faster than a flower.
Salt a bloodsucker, watch it cringe.
What hammer kills a tick?
We only alter what can hurt us.
The bears out back are terror.
"Let's build a big fire!"
Goddamn us herd of girls
out learning our power.

But I Had No Mother, No Friend

—*The Bondwoman's Narrative*, Hannah Crafts

Why would it interest anyone but me
that my life was charmed and rotten?

I'd love to never write
another poem about my life.

It might be possible to invent a place
like Wakefield, a post-mining/logging town on a copper lake.

Its open pit mines and underground mines collapsing,
rusting equipment, old loggers carving wooden spoons

and roosters outside the boarded temperance hall.
What had I? Sister and sister and sister,

candy father, prismatic mother, the ratty library on the hill.
Picture books then puberty's fizz and novels without pictures.

Mrs. Kiiskinen's sidelong gaze of a boarder guard
kept the clay dolls wearing costumes of Europe

captive in a case behind her desk.
We claimed the leather couches,

sucked jawbreakers and turned the grubby pages.
Down the hill our dentist, Doctor Bigford, drilled.

My sister was methodical,
crunching a stretchy candy necklace,

reading her way down
the row of Nancy Drews.

Hymen, erection, ejaculate . . .
words rose up like construction signs.

I read about testicles, one consolation.
Were these pink illustrations approximations

or as actual as a calendar?
The prose was vague and reverent

as though we would be conscripted
for a mystery the pages didn't reveal.

We headed for the matinee. Rock and Doris resting
on the headboard, smoking in a trance—

what had happened here?—
the puzzling ironed sheet folded on their chests.

In Wakefield I was coming to, but little
in my field of vision was clear.

One's Whole Dignity and Meaning

—*Lady Chatterley's Lover*, D.H. Lawrence

Open and unattended
is the bathhouse in the forest.

I've heard the spring has stalls
with carved-out cedar logs

where you soak in sulfur water
from volcanic fissures.

I'd love a ritual
like that.

A girl brings a thimble to a park picnic
with her friend to hem a party dress.

This is not a narrative,
it is an instance.

The girls eat cherries from a wrinkled sack
and spit the pits into the ravine.

Now a jogging man stops
and the oldest show begins.

One girl pretends to stitch,
the other looks as if she will be sick.

He's quick and gross and gone—
another jerk without a circle.

I'd feel more sorry
if I felt less slimed.

Connie Was Half Listening

—*Lady Chatterley's Lover*, D.H. Lawrence

Poor Connie crying over baby chicks, the kid she wants;
her troubled husband, a captain of industry;
and Mellors, the keeper. Classy problems.

The outside world never stills even when it's icy.
We say physical self, emotional self,
as though they could have an affair.

What belly has a root asks the urgent virgin,
reading in bed all day after the extraction—
the molars, bloody turnips drying on her nightstand.
The x-rays showed an oddity: a second set.
"They will descend," the dentist tells her twilight sleep.
She was feeling something true.

"What is a cunt?" Connie asks; "It's thee down theer; 'an what
I get when I'm i'side thee," explains the keeper.
Listen, the hole forgets the root.
Connie was not wise in the formal world,
yet she wants to be remembered.

Before the man made her want whole sex,
her favorite flower grew like low clouds in the woods,
a sexpot flower with a pale blue pucker,
the center, a baby sun.
She wants to be remembered.

Reading in bed all day, the girl's jaw ached
as she read about Connie and the keeper and their ravishment,
an ordinary separation eased by giving genitalia
royal names, by weaving belly flowers.

She Wore a Rabbit-Fur Coat

—Louisa, Simone Zelitch

The apex of uncool. A fur.
A January maybe, a not.
Not for one minute had she been hip,
an impossible posture, a great relief.

Beneath the heavy lining, hid
unmistakable skin,
the inside of a rabbit.
How many pelts does it take
to fashion a knee-length coat?

It was a dead woman's coat,
and the rabbits were also dead,
she reasoned, using what she had.

Holding a rabbit is frightening:
the twitching nose, the kicking chaos,
eyes red with plans.

When the neighbors' rabbits escaped
their hutch we used blankets
to snatch them in the rushes.

When poetry is prose, clothed
in the guise of lines,
can we forgive the fiction?

She wore the coat to college
in an upscale, liberal town.

Her boyfriend disdained her
lack of travel, her minor bourgeois ways.
"How can you live without
a garlic press?" moaned the empty bus.

She was cold; wrapped in fur
she was safe inside a pouch.

No one bombed her with blood.
No one rolled their eyes.
I don't know why.

In spring, she was safe enough inside
to shed the coat on the forest floor
and walk back in her hide.

For a Few Moments I Didn't Have a Single Sad Thought

—Hunger, Knut Hamsun

No wonder my fairy cousin shot
    her pink wad straddling a red hot poker.
        She says, "don't give them anything for free!"

I wish I had not seen the neck, skewer
    with a hinge, the long tongue meat,
        palsied claws pulled in.

These hummingbirds are summer verbs
    ready to erase each other. All sincerity
        and vice, bamboozlers with power tools,

their manners are impeccable, they trim the drop.
    Creepy sybarites with a sugar habit
        can push you out of thought.

Birch bark, gray moss, human hair spun
    into a little cup. I wish I had not
        looked into the nest and seen

the three pink gobs with pencil tip beaks
    that would not stop.
        One adult gets lift in the ivy

and riffs the shiny leaves,
    an unmysterious junky
        with hypodermic nerve.

You Cannot Hide the Soul

—*Moby Dick*, Herman Melville

I like the fourteen day divide, the moment
of ensoulment, when twins untie. Every soul

experiment says we lack the means of measure or
we've been living with a necessary lie. Meanwhile

we're inked to an addiction limited by space.
Students meditate the blue sea serpent

swimming up their yoga teacher's spine.
A sailor has a cross tattooed across his back.

No one would whip that! Unwrapped mummies show off
their tats. L-o-v-e and h-a-t-e the inmates prick. I know

whole lives worked in hiding the punctured stay of soul.
In-born or added, what abides, what bounces back?

The very subtle mind's not blurred by incarnations' deaths,
a continuum of ripening—human mammal—indelible you.

Notes

In "City of Roses" section VI contains my variations on the first line of Ovid's *Metamorphoses*.

The lines "Rise up out of sleep/get up out of dream" in "Resemblance" are from *The Kalevala*, Poem 15, "The Resurrection," by Keith Bosley, translator, 1989. "Resemblance" is a retelling of parts of Poems 14 and 15.

The lines "Blood, stand fast like a wall . . .Your place is in the heart" in "In the Gogebic Range" are from the *The Kalevala*, Poem 9, by Francis Peabody Magoun Jr., translator, 1963.

In "Daydream Three" the quotation is from William Blake's "The Crystal Cabinet," 1803.

The title of the section "The Reader Became the Book" is from Wallace Stevens's poem, "The House Was Quiet and the World Was Calm," 1947.

Acknowledgments

Antioch Review: "*There Was a Deer Whom the Carthean Nymphs Held Sacred*"
Ploughshares: "Note"

With special thanks to John Kuzma, Melissa Stevens, Lisa Vidigal, Antony Falco, Wendy Willis, William Olsen, Kimberly Kolbe, McKenzie Tozan and my family.

photo by Steve Bloch

Kathleen Halme's first book of poetry, *Every Substance Clothed*, was the winner of the University of Georgia Press Contemporary Poetry Series competition and the Balcones Poetry Prize. Her second collection, *Equipoise*, was published by Sarabande Books, and her third, *Drift and Pulse*, by Carnegie Mellon University Press. Her poems have appeared widely in journals, including *Ploughshares*, *Poetry*, *TriQuarterly*, *Boston Review*, and *Anthropological Quarterly*. Halme is a recipient of a National Endowment for the Arts Poetry Fellowship and a National Endowment for the Humanities Summer Fellowship in Anthropology. She grew up in Michigan's upper peninsula and now lives in Portland, Oregon.

The Green Rose Prize

2014:   Kathleen Halme
        My Multiverse

2013:   Ralph Angel
        Your Moon

2012:   Jaswinder Bolina
        Phantom Camera

2011:   Corey Marks
        The Radio Tree

2010:   Seth Abramson
        Northerners

2009:   Malinda Markham
        Having Cut the Sparrow's Heart

2008:   Patty Seyburn
        Hilarity

2007:   Jon Pineda
        The Translator's Diary

2006:   Noah Eli Gordon
        A Fiddle Pulled from the Throat of a Sparrow

2005:   Joan Houlihan
        The Mending Worm

2004:   Hugh Seidman
        Somebody Stand Up and Sing

2003:   Christine Hume
        Alaskaphrenia
        Gretchen Mattox
        Buddha Box

2002:   Christopher Bursk
        Ovid at Fifteen